Rebecca O'Connor grew up in Cavan in Ireland. She lived in the UK for ten years, and was a commissioning editor of literary fiction at Telegram Books in London. She won a Geoffrey Dearmer Prize in 2004 and was the recipient of a New Writing Ventures Poetry Award. Her chapbook *Poems* was published by the Wordsworth Trust, where she was a writer in residence in 2005. She returned to Ireland with her family in 2008, where she edits *The Moth* magazine.

We'll Sing Blackbird

Rebecca O'Connor

a *moth* edition

Copyright © Rebecca O'Connor 2012
ISBN 978-0-9569795-5-1

Published by
The Moth
The Bog Road
Dromard
Cavan
Ireland

www.themothmagazine.com

For my family

Contents

Write me a Drum	11
The Lakes	12
This is a true story about falling in love	13
Dear Taxidermist	15
Love	16
Shotgun	17
Magpie	18
Spring	19
Dream	20
A bag of tangerines	21
Accident Prone	22
Devil	23
First Holy Communion	24
Snail	25
May Day Wedding	26
French Exchange	27
Hide-and-seek	28
Studio	29
Daquise	30
This is a Boat	31
The Windjammer	32
Flick Book of Rain	33
Wet Dream	34
Hard of Hearing	35
Tiroler Hut	36
Storm	37
'My mind is a woman searching for her lost child'	38
All the Nothing	39
Magpies	40
Honeymoon	41
The Lyrebird	42

Domestic Bliss	43
Made in China	44
Fish Wife	45
Life After Death	47
Irish Language Lesson	48
Upstairs, Downstairs	49
The Winter's Cold	50
Road Trip	51
Dear Sally	52
Kapo	53
Birth of a Cow	54
A Year in Notes	55
'We stand at the window'	56
Thanks to Nicola Barker for the Yips	57
Note	58
Ember	59

Acknowledgements
Other *moth* editions

Write me a Drum

Here is its heart, a hollow that sings.
And here is its art – the taut tart *tat-te-tee-tat*.

The heart is rapt with such things. Here
it is, my heart. I would write you wood-
wind, brass, string, if I could –

an orchestra of rivers full of fish
playing waterfalls, kingfishers,
otters swimming.

The Lakes

The wet here can break a person's heart with sheer persistence.
Imagine one day your husband's beard smells of damp dog,
his long johns stink of pondweed, and you think nothing –
or very little – of it. Until, one day,
you wake to find him looking up at you with wet spaniel eyes.
That's what it's like – an endless incoming tide.
The trick is to give him plenty of exercise.

This is a true story about falling in love

Yesterday I said, 'Look! There's a parakeet!' and you said,
'No, that's a pigeon';
and I said, 'Look, there's a parakeet!'
and you said, 'No, that's a duck.'

It seems stupid now.

You said, 'This is a ratty bit,'
and there he was, big and fat.
Afterwards we saw squirrels shagging up a tree,
a Scots Pine.

It's difficult to write when you're in love.

First things first.
You told me there were crayfish in the Serpentine.

Secondly, you pointed out that the willows weeping into Long Water
looked like giant shaggy dogs stooping to drink.

That wasn't it.

Fishing with my brother's old rod in Killykeen, your line
snagged on a fist of freshwater mussels.

Now I'm worried you won't believe this:
that same weekend I saw my first double rainbow,
my first red squirrel, my first lunar eclipse.

We've watched the coots – from six down to two now – grow big,
a new nest of crisp packets and lollipop sticks.
We've stalked muntjac in the woods.

And last night
   a tawny owl ghosted through the park at dusk.

Dear Taxidermist

Out here past the adolescent River Erne, with your fish heads eyeing us
from the shelves – a two-headed lamb was once brought in to you
by a vet, you say, and a black bear by someone else.
If I had two heads I'd give one to you to mould and make good again,
make a gift of it to a friend, mounted on a piece of driftwood.
Instead I bring you this bullfinch,
bloodshot on the glass pane of the conservatory
where it mistook the reflection of the rowan tree for the real thing.
It's a wedding present. Strange, you say,
but beautiful all the same, as my second head would be,
given the right hands.

Love

And there they were,
the bitch fox and the he,
stuck, back to back,
in the middle of the field.
I never seen anything like it –
maybe for a few seconds maybe
in the ditch,
and then they'd disappear.
January, February time is when they mate, you see.
There was something in it ...

And then the hearse door not opening later,
refusing to open
so as I had to take my penknife
and cut out the glass pane
and get the coffin out that way ...

As if it was him saying, no,
I'm not ready.
And them foxes saying, look
this is the way it is.

Shotgun

They kept it in the bathroom
hooked above the soap dish.
The butt stock alone was good
to blunt the heads of pups;
bitches took a single shot.
He lifted it down, unpinned,
loaded and cocked it,
tipped back his imaginary cap,
pointed the gun at the fox,
slugging it through four walls –
over his sisters' beds, through the Sacred Heart,
his father's chair, the edge of the baby's cot
and into the bark of a tree.
Fox was dead.
And the bolt hurtled him against the sink,
knocking the first of his milk teeth.

Magpie

Hi, Mr Magpie.
I wasn't expecting to see *you*
… and it was going to be
such a
nice
day.
Rain? Sure.
And dark clouds.
Absolutely.
But nice in other ways ...
Now who knows,
Mr Magpie?
Only you do,
only you.

Spring

Just when we're losing all hope
a frog hops across the road.

And then another.
And then another.
And then another!

Oh man.
Man, dear, as the man said,
spring is here!

Just look at the way they stand,
mano-a-mano –

out there
in the dark and the wet and the wild,
the wipers going like billy-oh –

chins up, white chests throbbing
against the beam of the headlights.

Oh, but, oh, who'd stop them tonight!
On they go, from the winter woods
to the good life –
the one we've all been waiting for.

This one will be different.
This one will last forever.

Dream

You and I lie in a large cot.
The grinning bat hanging
from the bulb above us
flaps his wings
as the rat leans from the ceiling
to gnaw him from his perch.
A bird pecks at the rat.
Bees bump against the bird's wings.

A bag of tangerines

About a dozen tangerines
fell out of my blue shopping bag
and rolled down the bus aisle.
That made them smile,
though it was only a bag of tangerines
rolling down the aisle.

A gentleman in a white tunic
handed me four at a time,
the lady next to me stooped down
and scooped up a few,
the bus driver slowed right down:
'Are they limes?' 'No,
they're mandarins, tangerines –
a little bruised now.'

Accident Prone

Age three, he fell out of the window
watching *Danger Mouse*.
Eleven stitches.
Age four, he got the brunt of a golf club in the eye:
it swelled up like a bruised plum.
Five, nothing.
Age six, he was knocked down
at the zebra crossing in Tullamore.
Age seven, a wall in the back yard
was levered off his fractured leg
with a shovel.
Age eight, he came down with a strange bug
and was put in isolation
on the same ward as all the bald cancer kids in Dublin.
Age nine, his cheek swelled up:
a black stitch from an old wound was tweezed out.
Age ten, Dad got the local hard nut by the scruff,
urging him 'Come on, son. Hit him. Just once.'

Devil

My own reflection is still the most frightening thing.
I can see Him in my black eyes in the darkness –
worse even in the dusk. It doesn't help that I
watched *The Omen* when I was six –
not that there were mirrors in it, but crows.
Crows.
I'm still trying not to let them terrify me.
Them, and winter days.
And children called Damien.

First Holy Communion

Decked out in white socks, shoes, skirt,
blouse, gloves, parasol, bag and rosary beads
I received a wafer thin slice of the Body of Christ.
I was his lucky bride, and He was lucky to have me,
just turned seven and salivating.

The bread tasted of fever,
of His final words. Delicious.
I genuflected to the dark ceiling,
turned from the bishop to the pews,
salvation fizzing on my tongue, bit my lip –
one bright berry of blood on my satin shoe.

Snail

The snails are plump and white,
ripe for salt.
You unbuckle my red shoes,
loose my hair from its clasp

I
reach for your mouth.

May Day Wedding

Gorse fires are spreading in the west
as the newly weds nestle up to one another
in their replica Rolls Royce
and sip champagne in the shade of a rookery
where one of the fledglings is splayed
on a branch above its nest
like a feathery black kite.

This is the day that my baby,
a month shy of three,
does his first forward roll.
We've had so little rain
there is just dust under the bridge.

Later tonight, Bin Laden's feet
will be weighted down with stones.
Farmers will fill slurry spreaders with water
to quench flames.

French Exchange

It was somewhere northwest –
warmish, with a wispish Atlantic
in faded watercolours. I would have worn a cardigan,
if I wore cardigans then, as a girl of thirteen or fourteen.
Or – and, eating – it was outside, all Aurore's aunts
and baby cousins – and grandparents, maybe –
overlooking the water or plants or the beach.

The silent boy on crutches – I was silent too –
who I knew that I would love. Despite time,
the blank face, this desperately white page,
despite not knowing if I was really there
as the groom carried the bride around the lighthouse.

Hide-and-seek

You wouldn't know from looking at that photo
that we were in hiding. Sitting, bold as brass,
on that old green settee, baby brother on my knee,
big brother behind me, all playing hide-and-seek.
And Timothy, the absentee, counting to infinity.

Studio

I sat every Saturday and Sunday morning in that studio
   on All Saints Road.
Mai died suddenly in February. I didn't even get to give her
the kitch keyring I'd bought her in Cairo.
You walked with me down to Anna's boat.
She was six months pregnant at the time.
I climbed onto the bed beside her and held her close.
We smoked cigarettes on deck.
A coffin was chosen from the undertaker's brochure.
A few weeks later, I asked you to marry me.
You had a ring in the pocket of your coat.
We went to the gorilla enclosure at London Zoo the next day,
as that was where *you* had planned to propose.
Anna' daughter was born.
And one day the painting was finished.
My dress had changed colour. There was a beautiful strip
of wallpaper or fabric behind me instead of a blank wall.
The bone of my wrist shone white.
The ring was there on my finger.
And that was how it was, sitting still in that chair,
trying to fathom this new feeling
while keeping my eyes trained on the red geranium.

Daquise

The herring's curled on my plate like a fortune fish.
There's something good about this.
Something about the knives and forks,
the hands and knives and forks,
something good about slurping borsch.
You direct my eye to the mermaid
on the shelf behind me and my hand sticks
for a moment to the tablecloth.
I douse a slice of apple in sour cream.
The man beside me is drinking wine.
In my head I commend him for it.
Simply because it's Monday, and it's lunchtime,
and it's raining outside. Others, like me,
thought tap water good enough.

This is a Boat

We're adrift somewhere south of the Faroe Islands.
The blue floorboards creak with life.
You haul me onto the boat with your fishing hands.
A cold wind rattles the big window.
Something sounds way out at sea.
There is nothing we can do.
All we can see is a hoop of light
as we head due south
where our unborn child waits for us.

The Windjammer

Three pheasants on Holt Road shin through the ditch:
now it's not that far to the dark fudge of the saltings
below the crescents of kite and cabbage whites, the scratch
of cudweed under pines, scentless sea lavender
scrawling towards the dunes,
and you
up to your knees in luke-warm pools of minnow.
The glint of the windjammer's red sails, the shale underfoot –
these were meant to be for you.
    But there's a drowned boy on the beach.
        Further along a man filming his toddler
crawling out to sea.
Later
    I recall that you were born behind that window
        of slow-moving clouds
above the clematis roof, a thrush
dusting its feathers while ants rig green sails
above their heads, water spooling
through the pavement cracks towards your seat –
how a bird would have struck its beak against the bark
as it does now. How
suddenly this world was made ready for us both
without either of us knowing.
And side by side we lie
watching the dragonflies *zoot*
    from vine to vine
against a dimming sky.

Flick Book of Rain

The window is a turning page of swallows
in a flick book of rain, zipping right then slipping back
as the wind intensifies and whips everything flat.

A white cow shelters shyly by a bucket while the birds take turns
plucking above the telephone wires at the root of all the rain.
Another cow joins the first, and they move on,
tipping the bucket on its side as the rain subsides.

Wet Dream

I dream of tin cans – non-specific,
label-less. Just tin.
With that sound that tin cans can make when they
hit the ground.
Full tin cans, that is. Full
of I don't know what.
But whatever is in those tin cans has me in a spin.
I've never been so turned on.
Tens of tins, maybe
hundreds even,
all toppling at my feet,
and I can't
contain
myself.

Hard of Hearing

There was a school for the deaf
next to my bedsit on Rue St Jacques.

Quiet as winter;
the smell of bread.

Those lads didn't realise
that I got their crude hand gestures
better than I got French.

Tiroler Hut

We ordered two cold steins from the Heidi lookalike.
You were infatuated with the Ferris Bueller lookalike at the time.
You said, 'I wish I had a friend who'd go over there and tell him.'
So I went, minding not to knock over the cowbells being played
by the Pinnochio lookalike.

You were the only one who didn't look like someone else.

It happens to me more and more often – everyone I see
  resembles someone else.
Ferris Bueller lookalike's friend looked like a Specsavers model
I'd seen in a magazine. I smiled at him. He looked at my mouth.
The Pinnochio lookalike took out his Swiss horn.
It was like a scene from a John Irving novel.
That was another thing: places reminded me of other places I'd been.

The Ferris Bueller lookalike was boring.
We agreed we should leave without paying. Which reminded me
of two friends running from a Chinese takeaway with a cheeseplant
  years before.
The Heidi lookalike followed us out onto the street with the bill,
as we knew somehow she would.
You told her we'd forgotten …

I kept very still.
I was thinking about love, of what it was to take a taxi home together,
wondering if you and I might kiss some time,
and what that might mean.

Storm

... and if the wind should lift me
and carry me out to sea
I shall cast shadows
across your homeland
and your heart,
and scream with the wind, drowning
in the depths of the sea
that kept us apart,
drowning in the pool at Godmersham,
the Cork cove, under the cliffs
of the Bloody Foreland, the high rise car park
of the San Sebastian gravel and sands ...

My mind is a woman searching for her lost child.
My heart is a telephone in an empty foyer.
My hands are this line's apostrophe.
My insides are all the saints in heaven
praying for our lost souls.

All the Nothing

With the Icelandic waves rolling in my chest
and the sound of your steps on the snowy beach
I lay down to sleep last night
on my creased bed.

I dreamt you and I were a kiss:
time, all time. Then you made a sandcastle of yourself.
Later I plunged the depths
and couldn't see what anything meant –
just food for fish and smaller fish and smaller fish.

All I know now is,
even if I have nothing else,
I have this –
all the nothing that it is.

Magpies

Oh
  now look, there are two.
          Look!
She's shimmying up to him.
          Hi! Hello!
Yoo hoo!
          It's the twenty-fourth of June.
           We're sitting on the hotel lawn
          eating shortbread.
The lake is perfect ...
Oh joy!

Honeymoon

A hook full of worms is called a chandelier, according to my husband.
It's a week, and already I can't remember what it's like to be truly
  miserable.
The gannets dive-bomb the Atlantic as this thought occurs to me.
Out on the pier a young boy is telling a younger boy to *mind*,
loose the rope a little, pull the slack in.
In on the beach a man waits, knee-deep in water –
a tug-o-war with the net as it gives on to land,
the eels quicksilvering between the boys' hands –
three of them now, is it, or four.
And then another, who tells us *take some for bait if you want*.
I pick one up from the sand. My husband
plucks a tiny plaice from the net and puts it back in the sea.
The eldest boy is rowing out now. He's bringing the trawlers in
as we take to the barnacled rocks with our eels.

The Lyrebird

The lyrebird mimics the sound of the cross-cut saw
running along the forest floor.

If I was a bird, I'd mimic the sound of you coming to get me,
running across the corridor.

Domestic Bliss

I place a jug of lavender on the table
to mask the smell of mould from under the fridge

while you draw nails to hammer with your fist.
Then I draw a hammer, and watch

as you try to lift it from the page.
By day it's *Mr Men*, *Mad Men* by night,

your father and I wishing we could be so bold.
You have no such wants, though sometimes I wonder

as you try to peer into Jack and Jill's well
or climb the tiny ladder of your toy farm
to mend the red roof of your miniature barn.

Made in China

A man who works all day,
three-hundred-and-fifty-eight days a year,
a man with seven days in which to travel to his wife,
to make a family – what sort of man is he?

A man who makes bicycles.
A man who makes bicycles.
A man who makes bicycles.

A man who dreams of cogwheels,
three-hundred-and-sixty-five nights a year,
a man who dreams of high-speed gears
even as he lies next to his wife.

This man who makes bicycles.
This man who makes bicycles.
This man who makes bicycles.

A man who makes love like a dynamo bike,
six nights out of the year,
a man whose heart and head and prick
are like spokes on a spare-part wheel.

Dear man who makes bicycles.
Dear man who makes bicycles.
Dear man who makes bicycles.

Fish Wife

I recall falling asleep in the car while you gauged yet another
　　fishable body of water.
That was after spending an evening in the Poison Glen watching
　　you try to catch supper
while I cooked sausages on a disposable barbeque outside our
　　two-man tent.
I learned then – when I accidentally dropped your camera into
　　the lake while trying to fish out a bottle of champagne –
that you derived great pleasure from apportioning blame.
And that I bore easily.

My face was covered in midge bites for the duration of the honeymoon,
which I didn't seem to mind at the time.
It's only now, when I look at the photographs again,
　　that I see that I look sick.
By the end of it, I was glad to be returning to our bedsit in your
　　grandfather's apartment
with the vases of dried roses and the silent piano.
A month later I was pregnant.

I wish I could remember things better, get into the habit
　　of jotting things down,
but the first I have of it is standing on a bridge over Paddington Station
　　wanting to jump in front of a train.

And then we came here, a place I couldn't wait to leave,
and I must have cried for weeks, if you strung all the days,
the evenings together. I was so tired.

But people are kind.
We have trout in the freezer that a neighbour caught
  in Annagh Lake,
my parents' fold-up bed in the garage,
tulips from a friend on the kitchen table.
And I love you. I'm ready.

Life After Death

My thoughts are all opposed to that streak of red fox in the field,
black clods of thought that cling to the spade that lifts them
to throw them back into the hole they made.

The fox is an apposite thing, lived in without reluctance,
as is the greenfinch, even as it hits the window
and knocks itself out cold.

My child knows this. He won't allow himself forget
his father warming the bird's wings with his breath,
its sudden swift flight
as two foxes
   trot through Fayre's Field ahead of the hearse.

Irish Language Lesson

A typical *hello* would go something like this: May God and Saint Patrick and Mary and Joseph and Judas and Mother Teresa and Padre Pio and the Archangel Gabriel and Pope John Paul II and Lady Diana be with you.

To which one would typically reply: May God and Saint Patrick and Mary and Joseph and Judas and Mother Teresa and Padre Pio and the Archangel Gabriel and Pope John Paul II and Lady Diana and Peter Cook be with *you*.

After that it gets more complicated.

Upstairs, Downstairs

You stay below, painting swallows,
while I remain up here, wallowing in self pity.

The Winter's Cold

I cannot let go of the winter's cold.
Its memory is in the marrow.
This must be what it is to grow old –
to grow suspicious of the evenings closing in
even as the cuckoo sings.

The honeysuckle and the thistle in the hedgerow,
the sickle, the silo, gunshots from the bog,
nettles taller than I am, the dying hedgehog
in the patch of courgettes – all diminish into tomorrow.

How quickly the forget-me-not forgets the cuckoo flower,
the dandelion clocks, the primrose, snowdrops, snow.
I dress up, as I step indoors from the sun,
layering one thing over another to keep warm.

Road Trip

If you point out one more roadkill to me –
a fox, a mother and baby badger, a hedgehog –
I'll get out of this car and walk across the Irish Sea.
We're at Colwyn Bay now.
I've watched the fields of rapeseed turn to whin.
We've sung *Swim swim swimmy* to our baby until we could cry.
We've eaten pork pies and Pringles and Scotch eggs –
all before lunch.
I want to throw up. I'm hungry.
A single journey has turned me bulimic.
We stop at a garage so the dog can wee on the grass verge.
I show the baby some Welsh sheep.
I'm already looking forward to the salmon and brie sandwiches
  on the ferry.

Dear Sally

I haven't time for this.
But I'll make time.
There are sticks falling from the trees –
not leaves, but sticks.
Autumn usen't to be like this.
And furthermore, it *oughtn't*
to be like this.
I take issue, also, with
the paucity of rain.
All summer I've been waiting –
and all summer it rained –
and now this, a fall that's
taking the summer right up
to Christmas! Taking the piss
in this, the wettest, most dismal
of places normally.
Please explain.

Forlornly,
R. M. S.

Kapo

I'm reading about August Adam, would you believe –
Are you a lawyer? A professor?
Good! Do you see this green triangle?
This means I'm a killer,
and here I'm in command –
when I mistake the dock leaves in the field
for a flock of birds.
My husband and son go prancing past the window
to 'Jolene'. This cold May weather is strange.
I wouldn't know how to name it.
It's not depression, or loneliness.
I'm not lying, you know, when I say this:
Just now, I thought that flock of birds
was a heap of dock leaves in the field.

Birth of a Cow

The birth of the herd takes place in the back field
where we saw the hare last week.
The small black calf plies its suck to the teat
then lies with its red umbilical cord drying on the grass
while its bigger, identically black mother eats,
then licks her, eats, then licks.

The indifference of the cattle is marked by the static grey clouds
as they walk to the far end of the field.
They know no different, these cows. They chew –
another sign to the newborn to know what to do.

A Year in Notes

Extract from writing in progress – Harvest Moon – drawing group pic – Magpie/The Moth – Interviews: McCabe, Harding, etc. – Gatwick 18.40 – Ask Dermot Healy – buy InDesign – 13 July 2010, STOP SMOKING – Write about girl on train throwing up – email Nina, Orla, Sophie – Men wearing cheap cufflinks, girls with hair extensions, the smell of grubby kebab meat and chip grease, the empty streets – What services am I offering? – JUST YOUR TYPE (typewriter font) – Robert Sullivan, *New York Times* – Second Floor website – Johnny Cockfuller? – Where did she study? – Buy ISBNs – poem as song – could start 6th of June but would prefer 13/06 – would want to commute – the west/the sea – buttermilk, prawns, limes, ice, camembert, duvet – Write me a drum – email Jim – celebrating our first birthday – tractors/farmyard, bogeymen, etc. – holidays in Dingle June 2010 – I'm in London for three days – Powers Gold Label – My thoughts are all opposed to that streak of red fox – CLUTCH, BRAKE, GLANCE, LANE, MIRRORS, INDICATOR – I don't know, I just want to get back home

We stand at the window
singing the words to outside –
grass, reeds, crows, clouds …
You watch, long after I've spoken,
snow turn to ice water,
a hooded crow or a rook take flight,
a cloud's shadow move across the magnolia tree.

You are eight months old
and already you are the weight of the world to me.

Thanks to Nicola Barker for the Yips

I dandle the baby on my knee while I take a piss.
It's no joke. As I do so,
I notice the crevices of dirt in the linoleum.
'I'm just showing you this', the dentist
said to me yesterday, 'to get you flossing'
as she held before me a shard of bloody calculus
from between my bottom front teeth.
Honestly. Doesn't she know what I'm up against?
The dirt gives me the yips – makes me jittery for
drunk days, picnic-in-the-park days, after-dark days –
but it will stay there for now, where it is,
because baby is running a fever,
or at least I think he is.
His clothes feel damp to the touch.
He sucks and sucks.

My left hand has become conciliatory
and writes these lines for me
while baby lies propped up on my right,
his mouth questioning everything on the tongue.
I run my own tongue along the marble columns of my teeth
and feel pleased that they, at least, are clean.
There is not much else I can do at this stage
but be grateful for such small mercies.
Sometimes I kiss the baby *in* the mouth.
It's not filthy. Just love.

Note

I note beside your entry – *A fox cub on the road near Cloverhill* –
Nothing you haven't seen before: sparrows, a dunnock this morning.
Each day is simply a reminder of the one before.

The injured calf has gone to slaughter; the windows are so wet with dew
I can barely make out the rookery on the bare branches of the hilltop tree;
down at Deredis ice spawns around the lake's edge.

I'll take you to the spot where I saw two goldfinches, when you get back.
When you get back we'll sing 'Blackbird', I'll show you this.

Ember

The sky is the white smoke of a quenched fire,
and his heart is loose, poor George.
Peppa says he must stay in bed for three years,
which is what passes for a weekend here.

My heart too is loose, needs its noose tightened.
And just as I say this the sun seeps wetly through
to remind me that something smoulders,
something still burns.

Acknowledgements

Thanks to the editors of the following publications in which some of these poems appeared: *The Guardian*, *Jelly Bucket*, *Poetry Ireland Review*, *Poetry Review*, *The Spectator*, *Stand* and *The Stinging Fly*. And a special thanks to the Wordsworth Trust for publishing my pamphlet *Poems*, where some of these were first published.

Other *moth* editions

Some Poems by Ciarán O'Rourke
Some Poems by Dermot Healy
Some Poems by Kate Dempsey
Some Poems by Ted McCarthy

Available at www.themothmagazine.com